COMPUTER CODING WITH JAVASCRIPT

WORKBOOK

Authors and consultants

Alex Dytrych & Craig Steele

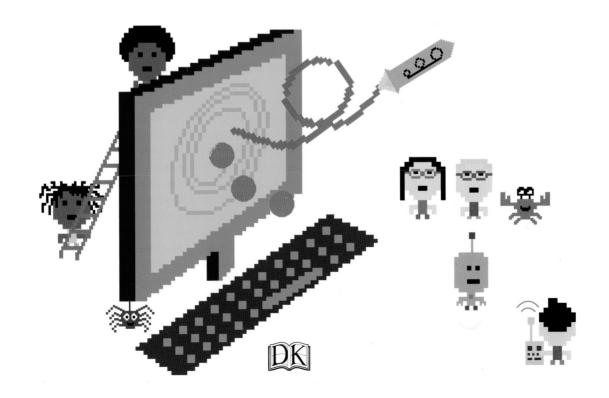

DK

Written by
Alex Dytrych & Craig Steele
Assistant Editor Prerna Grewal
Editor Jolyon Goddard
US Editor Margaret Parrish
Designer Peter Radcliffe
Project Art Editor Hoa Luc
Senior Art Editor Nidhi Mehra
Jacket Coordinator Francesca Young
Jacket Designers Dheeraj Arora, Amy Keast
Proofreader Kathleen Teece
Deputy Managing Art Editor Ivy Sengupta
Managing Editors Monica Saigal, Laura Gilbert
Managing Art Editor Diane Peyton Jones
Producer, Pre-Production Tony Phipps
Producers Basia Ossowska, Niamh Tierney
Art Director Martin Wilson
Publisher Sarah Larter
Publishing Director Sophie Mitchell

First American Edition, 2018
Published in the United States by DK Publishing
345 Hudson Street, New York, New York 10014

Copyright © 2018 Dorling Kindersley Limited
DK, a Division of Penguin Random House LLC
18 19 20 21 22 10 9 8 7 6 5 4 3 2 1
001–307948–Feb/2018

JavaScript™ is a registered trademark of Oracle America, Inc.
and/or its affiliates in the United States and other countries.

Thimble is Mozilla's free, browser-based tool for learning and teaching code. It has taught hundreds of thousands of people in dozens of
countries. As an open source project, Thimble is built by more than 300 contributors around the world. Thimble is also more than an educational
code editor—it's a creative platform. Thimble users can create personal web pages, comic strips, postcards, games, and more.

A catalog record for this book is available from the Library of Congress.
ISBN: 978-1-4654-6937-3

DK books are available at special discounts when purchased in bulk for sales promotions,
premiums, fund-raising, or educational use. For details, contact: DK Publishing Special Markets
345 Hudson Street, New York, New York 10014
SpecialSales@dk.com

Printed and bound in China

All images © Dorling Kindersley
For further information see: www.dkimages.com

A WORLD OF IDEAS:
SEE ALL THERE IS TO KNOW
www.dk.com

Contents

Meet JavaScript

Computers can't think for themselves. They need to follow sets of instructions called computer programs. Programs are written in computer programming languages. JavaScript is one of the most popular computer programming languages in the world.

What you'll learn:
• Computers run programs that tell them what to do
• Programs have to be written in special computer programming languages
• JavaScript, HTML, and CSS are languages used to make web pages
• JavaScript programs can be run using a web browser

Languages of the web

JavaScript is a computer programming language of the web. It works with other languages, such as HTML (HyperText Markup Language) and CSS (Cascading Style Sheets), to bring web pages to life and it lets you interact with them. For example, JavaScript code lets you play or pause a video on YouTube or choose which topping you want on your pizza when ordering online.

?

What topping do you want?

I know all about webs!

Easy to read

JavaScript is a text-based computer programming language. It uses a mixture of English words, symbols, and numbers. Learning to use it is a little like learning to read—once you know what the words and numbers mean, you can understand what is happening. Once you've picked it up, you'll soon be writing your own JavaScript programs!

Running the code

After you've written a JavaScript program, you need to run it using a web browser, such as Firefox, Chrome, or Safari. The browser uses a built-in tool called the JavaScript interpreter. The interpreter reads the code and follows its instructions, which might be something like adding numbers together or showing a picture on the screen.

Interactive projects you can share

This book features four interactive projects to work through that you can share with friends on web pages. The JavaScript code in this book showcases what this computer language was designed to do—let you interact with the screen and make fun games and projects.

Taking it further

Once you've become a JavaScript expert, you can look for other ways to use your new skill. Computer programmers don't just use JavaScript to build websites. They do other things with it, such as controlling robots, animating short films, or sending music to the speakers around their homes.

I am under your control!

How to use this book

This book starts you off coding in JavaScript, along with some basic HTML. Follow the steps carefully to create your own fun JavaScript projects. Once you've completed the project you'll be able to tweak or remix your code to create your own unique version. If you get stuck, you can move on to another project and come back to it later—the more practice you get the easier coding will be.

Using Thimble

You can use a tool called Thimble to write the code for the projects in this workbook. Thimble is a code editor made by the Mozilla Foundation that lets you write JavaScript, HTML, and CSS code easily.

What you'll learn:
• You can use Thimble to write JavaScript, HTML, and CSS code
• What Thimble looks like and what the different parts of it do or show you

Type in the name of your project here

Click here to create a new file

Your files are stored here. To edit a file, click its name on the list below

Clicking here will show you the HTML file

The gray areas are much darker on-screen. Code appears in several colors, depending on the types of command that you use

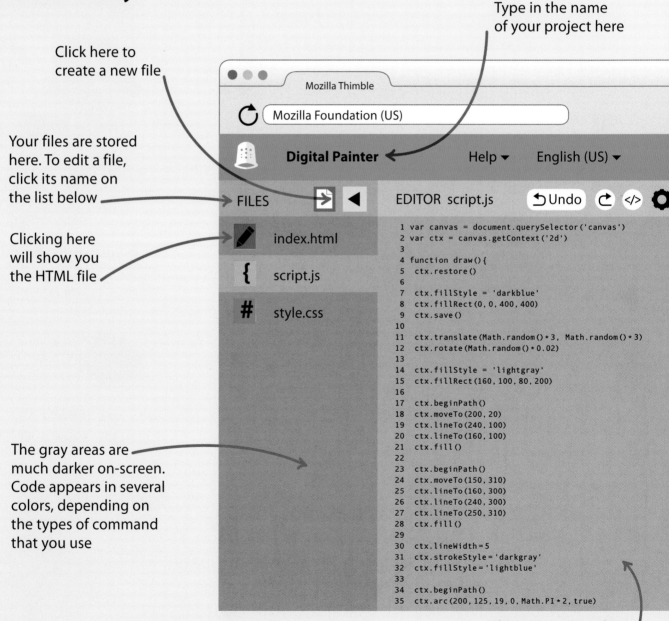

Mozilla Thimble

Mozilla Foundation (US)

Digital Painter   Help ▾   English (US) ▾

FILES

index.html

script.js

style.css

EDITOR script.js   ↺ Undo ↻ </> ⚙

```
 1 var canvas = document.querySelector('canvas')
 2 var ctx = canvas.getContext('2d')
 3
 4 function draw(){
 5  ctx.restore()
 6
 7  ctx.fillStyle = 'darkblue'
 8  ctx.fillRect(0, 0, 400, 400)
 9  ctx.save()
10
11  ctx.translate(Math.random()*3, Math.random()*3)
12  ctx.rotate(Math.random()*0.02)
13
14  ctx.fillStyle = 'lightgray'
15  ctx.fillRect(160, 100, 80, 200)
16
17  ctx.beginPath()
18  ctx.moveTo(200, 20)
19  ctx.lineTo(240, 100)
20  ctx.lineTo(160, 100)
21  ctx.fill()
22
23  ctx.beginPath()
24  ctx.moveTo(150, 310)
25  ctx.lineTo(160, 300)
26  ctx.lineTo(240, 300)
27  ctx.lineTo(250, 310)
28  ctx.fill()
29
30  ctx.lineWidth=5
31  ctx.strokeStyle='darkgray'
32  ctx.fillStyle='lightblue'
33
34  ctx.beginPath()
35  ctx.arc(200, 125, 19, 0, Math.PI*2, true)
```

This area is the editor, where you write your JavaScript (shown here), HTML, or CSS code

Getting started on Thimble

You'll need the latest version of a web browser, such as Firefox or Chrome, on your computer. Go to Thimble's home page (**https://thimble.mozilla.org**) and click on **Start a project from scratch** to begin.

Other code editors

There are other online code editors for writing JavaScript, HTML, and CSS code—you might want to try out **JSFiddle** or **CodePen**, too. They look a little different from Thimble, but you'll soon get the hang of them.

You don't need to save your code. Click here and the preview page will update immediately

You can create an account to store your work, but Thimble also works without one. However, you'll need an account to save and publish your project for others to see

Sign in or Create an account to Save and < Publish

When you're working on your project, only you can see it. If you click on **Publish**, you'll get a link to share it with friends

PREVIEW ☑ AUTO

The page will update automatically as long as this box is checked

Click here to make the preview page the full size of your screen

Click here to see what your project would look like on a smartphone

You can change the size of the editor panel and preview page in Thimble by dragging the edges

Your project will appear automatically on this preview page. It will look like this as a web page

Digital Painter

Learn to use JavaScript to paint your own digital masterpiece. See how you can use code to create a picture of a rocket ship from basic shapes. You'll then use simple code to make it look like it's soaring through the sky!

What you'll learn:
- How to set up a canvas using HTML and JavaScript
- How to draw using JavaScript
- How to make a simple animation effect

This square is your canvas

You'll write code to create simple shapes that build up the rocket

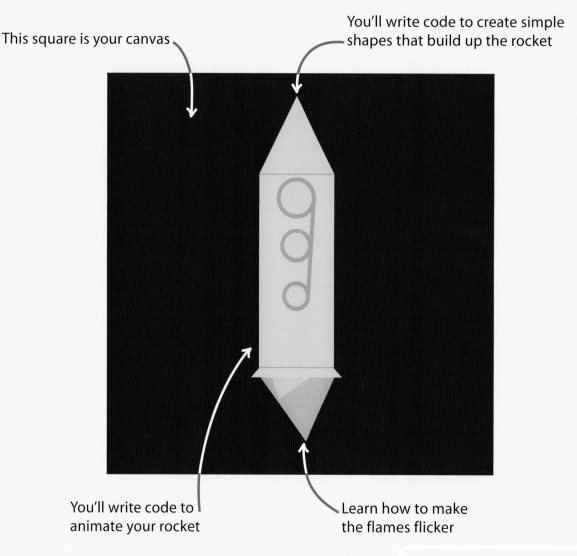

You'll write code to animate your rocket

Learn how to make the flames flicker

▲ What you do

In this project, you'll build a page with HTML and then "paint digitally" using JavaScript. Throughout this book, HTML code is shown on a gray grid and JavaScript code on a bluish grid.

HTML

JavaScript

Starting with a canvas

In all the projects in this book, we first need to code in HTML before we code in JavaScript. HTML lets us put words on the page and set up a canvas on which we can paint our rocket ship.

Copy the code in black!

In each step, you need to copy the code shown in black. Gray code is code that was already in the file, or code that you wrote in earlier steps and don't need to type in again. It's there to show you exactly where the new code fits in.

1 Let's start by creating a new project in Thimble. Go to **thimble.mozilla.org** in your web browser and click **Start a project from scratch**.

✎ **Start a project from scratch**

Click here to begin **Digital Painter**

2 On the right of Thimble is a preview of what your web page looks like, and on the left you'll write code. Thimble's added some HTML code for you automatically. Keep this, but change the words **Welcome to Thimble** to **Digital Painter** and delete **<p>Make something amazing with the web!</p>**. What happens?

HTML elements begin with an opening tag, such as **<h1>**, and a closing tag, such as **</h1>**. The **h1** element is the code for the page's main heading

```
<body>
    <h1>Digital Painter</h1>
</body>
```

HTML and elements

Hyper**T**ext **M**arkup **L**anguage (HTML) is the coding language that every website is written in. It is made up of **elements**. HTML code is used for the content, or words and pictures, on the page. An element is a single thing on a page, such as a paragraph, heading, or image. In the code for step 2, there is a **body** element, which contains all the web page's content, and an **h1** element, which is the page's main heading. In step 2, we'll add a **canvas** element. This creates an empty image that we can draw on using JavaScript code.

Elements not elephants!

3 Just like a real painter, our **Digital Painter** needs a blank canvas to bring to life with colors and shapes. We can add a canvas to our HTML and paint on it later using JavaScript code. Add this code to the HTML file, above the closing **body** tag.

The canvas will be a square measuring 400 by 400 pixels. Pixels are the tiny dots that make up your screen's display

```
<body>
    <h1>Digital Painter</h1>
    <canvas width="400" height="400"></canvas>
</body>
</html>
```

4 Before we get to the exciting part of the project—using JavaScript—we need to tell our HTML file that we're going to add a JavaScript file. After our **canvas** element, we can add another element called **script**. This tells the browser to load a new JavaScript file, which we're about to create. Add this code.

You'll notice that Thimble uses predictive text, or autocomplete, which helps you type the code faster

```
    <canvas width="400" height="400"></canvas>
    <script src="script.js"></script>
  </body>
</html>
```

Welcome to JavaScript!

In this project, we'll use JavaScript to paint a rocket ship and animate it, or make it move, a little. In the other projects, we'll use JavaScript to make interactive features.

Click to create a JavaScript file

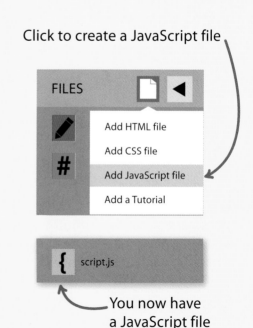

You now have a JavaScript file

5 Now we need to add some JavaScript. Click on ☐, to the right of **FILES**, and choose **Add JavaScript file** from the drop-down list. Just like the HTML file, Thimble has given us some code automatically. We don't need it though. Delete it so the file is completely empty.

6 The JavaScript and HTML files are now linked, so we can start writing some JavaScript. We first need to tell JavaScript about our canvas. Add the code below. It creates two variables: **canvas**, which remembers our **canvas** element, and **ctx**, which remembers something called the **context**.

Variables

A **variable** is used to store information that we need in our program. Every variable has a **name** and a **value**. The value stored in the variable can be changed or updated. For example, a game might have a variable called **score**. When the game starts, score would be set to **0**. The variable would then be updated each time the player gets a point. At the end of the game, the variable holds the player's final score.

```
var canvas = document.querySelector('canvas')
var ctx = canvas.getContext('2d')
```

If the canvas is the surface we're painting on, the context is the painter. We give the context instructions such as **Use red!** and **Draw a box!** and the context paints on the canvas

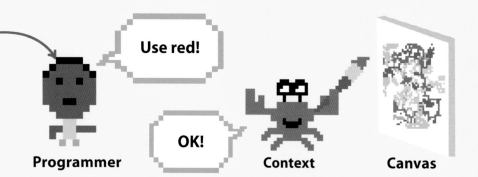

Use red!

OK!

Programmer　　**Context**　　**Canvas**

7 Let's start painting! Add the code below and then refresh the preview page by clicking on ↻. You may have to click a few times to get it to refresh. You should see a dark-blue square appear on the page. Try changing the color to **'pink'** or **'seagreen'**. What happens when you change the numbers in **fillRect**? Press ↻ again to see what it looks like.

```
var ctx = canvas.getContext('2d')

function draw() {
  ctx.fillStyle = 'darkblue'
  ctx.fillRect(0, 0, 400, 400)
}

draw()
```

We set the **fillStyle** to **'darkblue'** and then tell the context to paint a square rectangle in that color over the whole canvas

This section of code, called **draw**, is where we'll put all our instructions telling the context how to paint a rocket ship on the canvas

8 Time to start making our rocket! On the canvas, we can build pictures from simple shapes and lines. Let's add another rectangle to be the main body of the rocket. Add this code, and refresh it to check it works.

```
ctx.fillStyle = 'darkblue'
ctx.fillRect(0, 0, 400, 400)

ctx.fillStyle = 'lightgray'
ctx.fillRect(160, 100, 80, 200)
}

draw()
```

fillStyle sets the color on the painter's brush

fillRect paints the rectangle

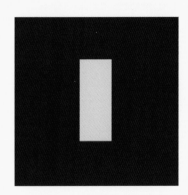

9 Now we have the body of our rocket, we need a pointed triangle for the nose at the top. Our canvas doesn't know how to draw triangles though, so we need to tell it how. Add this code, and click on ↻ to refresh.

```
ctx.fillRect(160, 100, 80, 200)

ctx.beginPath()
ctx.moveTo(200, 20)
ctx.lineTo(240, 100)
ctx.lineTo(160, 100)
ctx.fill()
}

draw()
```

Finally, we fill in the shape

This code tells the context how to draw a triangle on the canvas. The command **beginPath** starts the shape and draws lines between the coordinates below

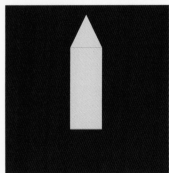

Coordinates

Coordinates give a position by saying how far left or right and up or down something is. The coordinates we're using in this project might be a little different from the ones you've seen before as the vertical number, or **y-coordinate**, goes down instead of up. It measures how far something is from the top of the canvas. The **x-coordinate** measures how far something is from the left edge of the canvas and is always written first.

0   X

●(x: 5, y: 2)

●(x: 4, y: 8)

●(x: 7, y: 12)

Y

10 We can do the same thing to draw the base of the rocket, where the flames will shoot out from. Add this code and refresh the preview page.

```
ctx.lineTo(160, 100)
ctx.fill()

ctx.beginPath()
ctx.moveTo(150, 310)
ctx.lineTo(160, 300)
ctx.lineTo(240, 300)
ctx.lineTo(250, 310)
ctx.fill()
}

draw()
```

This code adds a trapezoid to make the rocket's base

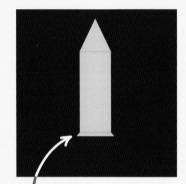

We now have our basic rocket shape with just three shapes

11 How about we add some windows for the astronauts to see out of? Otherwise, they might have a hard time steering the rocket! First, let's get our digital paintbrushes ready with this code.

The windows will be drawn with a dark-gray outline that's five pixels thick. They will be filled in with light blue

```
ctx.lineTo(250, 310)
ctx.fill()

ctx.lineWidth = 5
ctx.strokeStyle = 'darkgray'
ctx.fillStyle = 'lightblue'
}

draw()
```

Hurry up with those windows!

12 Time to draw those windows! The code you need to write may look complicated, but it's just telling the context to draw three circles, which will be our windows.

Our rocket ship is now ready for takeoff!

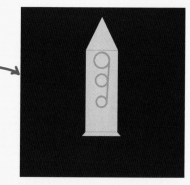

The first three numbers in each **arc** command are the x- and y-coordinates of the circle's center and the radius

```
    ctx.fillStyle = 'lightblue'

    ctx.beginPath()
    ctx.arc(200, 125, 19, 0, Math.PI * 2, true)
    ctx.arc(200, 175, 17, 0, Math.PI * 2, true)
    ctx.arc(200, 225, 15, 0, Math.PI * 2, true)
    ctx.fill()
    ctx.stroke()
}

draw()
```

13 Our rocket is starting to really look like something, but it isn't going anywhere yet. Let's add some flames at the bottom. We'll draw two more triangles—one orange and one yellow.

Just like when we were drawing shapes before, we use **beginPath** and **fill**. The **arc** commands draw the circles and **stroke** draws the outline

```
    ctx.stroke()

    ctx.fillStyle = 'orange'
    ctx.beginPath()
    ctx.moveTo(160, 310)
    ctx.lineTo(200, 370)
    ctx.lineTo(240, 310)
    ctx.fill()

    ctx.fillStyle = 'yellow'
    ctx.beginPath()
    ctx.moveTo(180, 310)
    ctx.lineTo(200, 330)
    ctx.lineTo(220, 310)
    ctx.fill()
}

draw()
```

Two triangles create the look of flames

14 Ignition time! Let's bring our picture to life by making the flames move. We'll tweak the JavaScript code we've already written so that the shape of the fire triangles change 33 times a second. That creates a simple fire animation. Change your code like this.

Delete some of the earlier code, shown crossed out in the three green bands, and add the new black code

```
ctx.lineTo(200, 370)
  ctx.lineTo(180 + Math.random() * 30, 350 + Math.random() * 40)
  ctx.lineTo(240, 310)
  ctx.fill()

  ctx.fillStyle = 'yellow'
  ctx.beginPath()
  ctx.moveTo(180, 310)
  ctx.lineTo(200, 330)
  ctx.lineTo(190 + Math.random() * 20, 320 + Math.random() * 20)
  ctx.lineTo(220, 310)
  ctx.fill()
}

draw()
setInterval(draw, 30)
```

15 Blast off! Our rocket is complete and the engine is firing. Let's finish by adding some movement to our rocket to make it look like it's hurtling through the sky. Carefully insert these four lines of code near the start of the **draw** section.

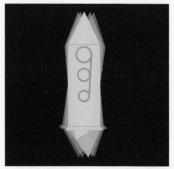

SetInterval redraws our painting every 30 milliseconds

Here, we're using **translate** and **rotate** to move and turn our painting a little each time it's redrawn

```
function draw() {
  ctx.restore()

  ctx.fillStyle = 'darkblue'
  ctx.fillRect(0, 0, 400, 400)

  ctx.save()
  ctx.translate(Math.random() * 3, Math.random() * 3)
  ctx.rotate(Math.random() * 0.02)

  ctx.fillStyle = 'lightgray'
```

Show what you know

1. What do the letters HTML stand for?

H .... T .... M .... L ....

2. Circle the correct answer.

The **canvas** / **variable** is an empty space we can paint on. Javascript code tells the **element** / **context** what to paint.

3. Match these canvas functions to their definitions.

`fillRect`   Outline a shape

`beginPath`   Move the pen without drawing a line

`moveTo`   Start drawing a shape

`stroke`   Color in a rectangle

4. Fill in the blanks in this sentence using the words below it.

A .... is used to store .... that we need in our ....

information   **program**   **variable**

5. Which shape does this code draw? Try to draw it on paper to help you.

```
ctx.beginPath()
ctx.moveTo(100, 50)
ctx.lineTo(150, 150)
ctx.lineTo(100, 250)
ctx.lineTo(50, 150)
ctx.fill()
```

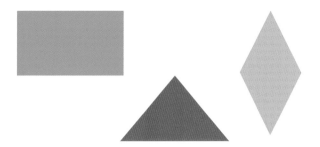

a. Rectangle   **b.** Diamond   **c.** Triangle

Magic Mirror

You can use JavaScript to control your webcam and create a crazy magic mirror. Make your face appear on the screen, and then use code to change the color, make it blurry, or turn yourself into a work of art!

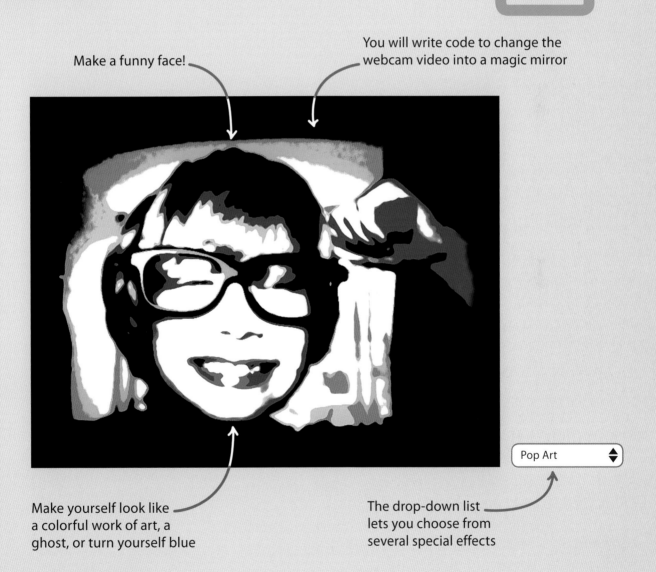

Make a funny face!

You will write code to change the webcam video into a magic mirror

Pop Art

Make yourself look like a colorful work of art, a ghost, or turn yourself blue

The drop-down list lets you choose from several special effects

▲ What you'll do

For this fun activity, you will code with JavaScript and HTML. Once you've written the code, just look into the webcam and make the funniest face you can! Use the drop-down list to switch between different special effects.

Start with HTML

You'll need to write some HTML code in the first few steps of this project. The HTML builds the structure of the page. We'll then use JavaScript to make our **Magic Mirror** interactive!

1 Create a new project in Thimble. If you need a reminder on how to do this, see step 1 of **Digital Painter** (page 9).

2 Let's give the project a heading and instructions. In the HTML file, delete the words **Welcome to Thimble** and **Make something amazing with the web!** after the line that says **<body>**. Then, replace them with the text in black, below.

This shows a heading on the page

This is a **paragraph** element. It's an easy way to show text on the page

```
</head>
<body>
  <h1>Magic Mirror</h1>
  <p>
    Choose a special effect and make a silly face!
  </p>
</body>
```

3 After the **paragraph** element, add a **video** element. We use this element to put video onto a web page. Nothing will show here now, but it's where we'll send the video from our webcam later.

You'll soon notice that coding with Thimble uses predictive text, or autocomplete, which can help you type it in faster

```
<body>
  <h1>Magic Mirror</h1>
  <p>
    Choose a special effect and make a silly face!
  </p>
  <video autoplay></video>
</body>
```

4 We now need to connect the HTML file to a JavaScript file. In the HTML file, add this line of code after the **video** element.

This line connects the HTML file to a JavaScript file that we're now going to create

```
  <video autoplay></video>
  <script src="script.js"></script>
</body>
```

Setting up the webcam

We're now ready to write some code in JavaScript. It will make the video stream from the webcam appear on the page.

5 Create a new JavaScript file by choosing **Add JavaScript file** from the **document** menu. A new file called **script.js** will appear in your documents. Thimble will automatically add in some sample code into your new file, but you should delete it so the file is blank.

6 Add this code as the first line in your JavaScript file. It gets the **video** element from the HTML page and remembers it in a variable called **video**.

We need to store the location of the **video** element in a variable. That means whenever we write **video** in our code, JavaScript will know what we're talking about

```
var video = document.querySelector('video')
```

7 Next, add this code below the first line of your JavaScript file. It tells the computer that we want to access the webcam and display it in the **video** element.

This code asks permission to use your webcam video

```
var video = document.querySelector('video')

navigator.mediaDevices
  .getUserMedia({
    video: true,
  })
  .then(function (stream) {
    video.srcObject = stream
  })
```

If you give permission, your webcam video will be streamed onto your preview page

Webcam permission

When you work through this project, you may get a message, like the one shown here, asking for permission for Thimble to use your webcam. If you click **Allow**, you give Thimble permission to use it. Thimble is safe and won't record you. If you visit other websites and this box pops up, click **Block** or ask an adult if you're not sure it's safe.

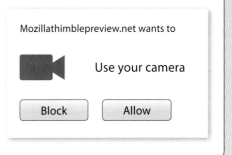

Mozillathimblepreview.net wants to

Use your camera

Block   Allow

8 Now it's time to test your code. Click on ↻ to refresh Thimble. Once the code has been run, you'll see your webcam video displayed on your page. If it's not working, go back and check your code carefully for mistakes and try again. Is it there? Brilliant! Now you're ready to add special effects to the video.

Special effects

We'll now add code for special effects, which are made by filters that change what you see on the video. We'll also write code that lets you change between the effects by using a drop-down list.

Lights! Camera! Action!

9 We now want to be able to choose an effect from a drop-down list. Go into your HTML file and type in this code after the **video** element.

The **select** element is used to create a drop-down list

```
<video autoplay></video>
<select>
  <option value="">Choose an effect</option>
  <option value="blur(10px)">Blur</option>
  <option value="contrast(500%)">Contrast</option>
</select>
<script src="script.js"></script>
```

Remember you need a closing **select** tag here

Each item in the list is an **option** element

10 Now we need to write code to make the video change depending on the special effect you choose. In your JavaScript file, insert this line of code immediately after the **video** variable. This gets the **select** element from the HTML file, so that we can talk about it later in our JavaScript code.

This code stores the **select** element in a variable called **select**

```
var video = document.querySelector('video')
var select = document.querySelector('select')
```

11 Now add this code. It makes a function that changes the filter effect on the video to whatever we choose in the **select** element. If we choose **Blur**, it adds the **blur(10px)** filter that we added to our HTML code in step 9 to the video.

```
var select = document.querySelector('select')


function changeEffect() {
  video.style.filter = select.value
}
```

12 Finally, add the last piece of code. It says that whenever the **select** variable changes, which happens when we click on the drop-down list and pick a new effect, we should run the **changeEffect** code we added in step 11.

```
function changeEffect() {
  video.style.filter = select.value
}
select.addEventListener('change', changeEffect)
```

Event listeners

In step 12, we added an **event listener**. This is a special piece of code that runs when something else, known as an **event**, happens. An event might be clicking a button, pressing a key, or defeating an enemy in a game. In this project, the event is changing the effect on the drop-down list. The event listener then changes the filter so we see the effect we just chose.

I've always wanted to appear on-screen!

13 Test your code by running it and switching between the two different effects. Which do you prefer—the vague, misty **Blur** option or the intense colors of the **Contrast** option?

That's the silliest face you've made yet!

PREVIEW ○ ☑ AUTO

Magic mirror

Choose a special effect and make a silly face!

Choose a special effect from the drop-down list

Contrast ⬍

14 If you want more crazy effects, try adding these seven extra options to your HTML file. Maybe you can figure out how to add some more options of your own.

Try changing some of the numbers in the options. Refresh the code to see what this does

```
<option value="contrast(500%)">Contrast</option>
<option value="hue-rotate(90deg)">Color 1</option>
<option value="hue-rotate(180deg)">Color 2</option>
<option value="hue-rotate(270deg)">Color 3</option>
<option value="invert(100%)">Invert</option>
<option value="grayscale(100%)">Black and white</option>
<option value="hue-rotate(180deg) invert(100%)
grayscale(50%)">Ghost</option>
<option value="blur(2px) brightness(100%) contrast(1000%)
saturate(1000%) hue-rotate(200deg)">Pop Art</option>
</select>
```

Show what you know

1. Circle the correct answers.

a. You can use the **getUserMedia** / **getUserCamera** command in JavaScript to ask for permission to use your webcam.

b. By adding a **layer** / **filter** to the video you can create your own special effects.

2. Draw a line to connect each piece of code to its description.

`contrast(10%)`   Makes the image completely black

`invert(100%)`   Makes the colors appear faint or washed out

`grayscale(100%)`   Reverses the colors in the video

`brightness(0%)`   Makes the video black and white

3. You can add this code as a new option. How would you describe the result?

```
<option value="sepia(100%)">Sepia</option>
```

4. Find the bug, or mistake, in this block of code.

```
<select>
  <option>Cola</option>
  <option>Lemonade</option>
  <option>Apple Juice<option>
  <option>Water</option>
</select>
```

5. In JavaScript, what do we use when we want the program to wait for something to happen, such as pressing a button, before running a certain part of the code?

a. Event listener **b.** Event watcher **c.** Event speaker

Tug-of-war

Find out who has the fastest finger in this keyboard-mashing tug-of-war game! Compete against a friend to see who can "tug" the red dot into their side of the line.

What you'll learn:
• How to reuse code with **functions**
• How to add arguments to **functions**
• How to make decisions in your code with **if statements**

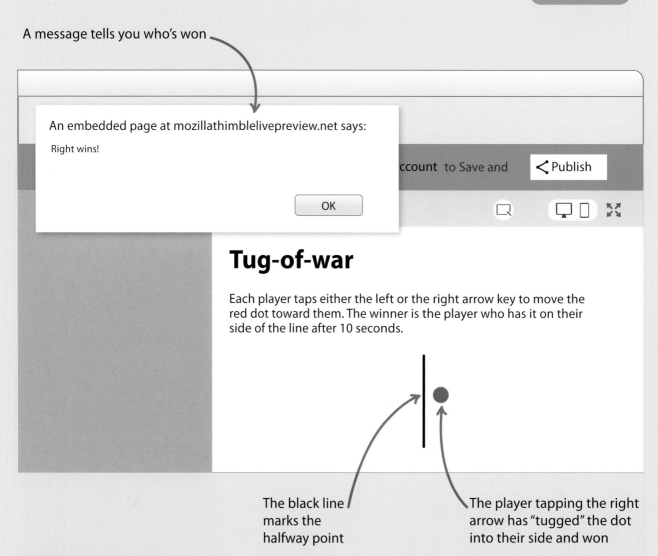

A message tells you who's won

An embedded page at mozillathimblelivepreview.net says:

Right wins!

OK

...ccount to Save and

‹ Publish

Tug-of-war

Each player taps either the left or the right arrow key to move the red dot toward them. The winner is the player who has it on their side of the line after 10 seconds.

The black line marks the halfway point

The player tapping the right arrow has "tugged" the dot into their side and won

▲ What you do

In this project, you'll code in JavaScript and HTML. Always type the code in very carefully. Also, make sure you put the code in the correct file and in the correct place or the program won't work.

Getting started

As in our other projects, we'll first write some HTML code, which will add words to our page. HTML also lets us set up a canvas, so we can then switch to JavaScript to draw the components of the game.

Let's have a tug-of-war!

1 Start a new project in Thimble. We'll begin by editing the code in the HTML file. Make the changes shown below. We'll add a title, instructions, and **canvas** and **script** elements, as we did in **Digital Painter**.

The name of our game is in the **h1** element and will appear as the title of our page

```html
<body>
    <h1>Tug-of-war</h1>
    <p>
    Each player taps either the left or the right arrow
key to move the red dot toward them. The winner is the
player who has it on their side of the line after 10
seconds.
    </p>
    <canvas width="500" height="100"></canvas>
    <script src="script.js"></script>
</body>
```

Tug-of-war

Each player taps either the left or the right arrow key to move the red dot toward them. The winner is the player who has it on their side of the line after 10 seconds.

Your project's title and the instructions will appear on the preview page

2 Create a new JavaScript file (see page 10). Delete what's already in it. Copy the code below to get the **canvas** element set up.

The context will paint on the canvas

```javascript
var canvas = document.querySelector('canvas')
var ctx = canvas.getContext('2d')
```

3 We need to add two variables (see page 11) that we'll use later in the game. Type these two lines of code into your file.

The variable **middle** remembers where the middle of our canvas is. In step 1, we set the **width** to 500 pixels, so its middle is 500 ÷ 2 = 250 pixels across

```
var canvas = document.querySelector('canvas')
var ctx = canvas.getContext('2d')

var middle = 250
var position = middle
```

The variable **position** remembers how far left or right the dot has been moved. We want it to start in the center, so we set it to **middle**

Drawing the components

The components of this game are pretty easy to draw—just a line and a red dot. We'll also add JavaScript code that moves the ball, keeps time, and tells you who has won.

4 Let's now draw our scene. Add this section of code called **draw**.

Draw is a **function**. Whenever we say **draw** later in our code, it knows to run the lines between the { } brackets

In the function, we first clear a rectangle so our canvas is empty

```
var middle = 250
var position = middle

function draw() {
  ctx.clearRect(0, 0, 500, 100)

  ctx.beginPath()
  ctx.moveTo(middle, 0)
  ctx.lineTo(middle, 100)
  ctx.stroke()
}

draw()
```

The last part of our code runs the **draw** function. Try running the code with and without that last line—what's the difference?

Then we draw a line as a marker down the middle of the screen

Refresh your page. A vertical line should appear

Functions

A **function** is small section of code that performs a useful task. We give it a **name**, and we can then use just the name to do the task again. That way we don't have to rewrite all the code. Imagine a cake recipe where each time you needed to mix the ingredients, it explained how to pick up a spoon, put it in the bowl, and move it around in a circle. The recipe would be so long! Think of **mix** as a function. If we teach our code what it means, we then don't need to write its code in full the next time we want to mix the ingredients.

Don't use that long recipe, just mix!

5 Let's add a little red dot to play tug-of-war with. Carefully slot in these four lines of code after the line **ctx.stroke()** from step 4.

```
ctx.lineTo(middle, 100)
ctx.stroke()

ctx.beginPath()
ctx.fillStyle = 'red'
ctx.arc(position, 50, 5, 0, Math.PI * 2)
ctx.fill()
}

draw()
```

Tug-of-war

Each player taps either the left or the right arrow key to move the red dot toward them. The winner is the player who has it on their side of the line after 10 seconds.

During the game, each player will "tug" on the red dot

6 In addition to drawing the middle line and the red dot, we also need to be able to move the dot left and right. Let's add another function to our code. This new function changes the position of the red dot and runs **draw** to update the screen. Right now this won't do anything—you'll have to wait until step 8!

I can't get it to move!

```
draw()

function move(distance) {
  position = position + distance
  draw()
}
```

This function is called **move**. It has one argument called **distance**

Arguments

Arguments don't mean that our function is going around getting into fights! In JavaScript, a function's arguments are extra bits of information that help the function know what to do. For example, rather than saying just **mix** in a cake recipe, we might say **mix for 5 minutes**. Here, **5 minutes** is the argument, telling you how long to mix.

We need to have an argument!

7 Let's add an **event listener** to the end of our file (see page 21). We'll then be able to move the dot when the players press the arrow keys.

```
  position = position + distance
  draw()
}

window.addEventListener('keydown', function (event) {
  event.preventDefault()
})
```

This **event listener** runs a special function called **preventDefault**. This stops the computer from doing its usual job when a key is pressed, such as scrolling the page up, down, left, or right

8 Add the code below, placing it above the line **})** (a closing bracket and a closing parenthesis) from step 7. Test it by clicking on the preview page and then tapping the right arrow key. Does the dot move? If not, check your code carefully. Make sure you have the right symbols and are using capital letters in the correct places.

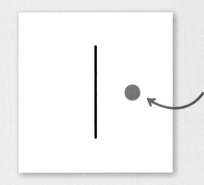

Pressing the right arrow key should move the dot 10 pixels to the right

```
}

window.addEventListener('keydown', function (event) {
  event.preventDefault()

  if (event.key === 'ArrowRight') {
    move(10)
  }
})
```

These lines of code say that if the key pressed is the right arrow, move the dot 10 pixels to the right

=== (three equals signs) means **is the same as**

An **if statement** lets our code ask a true/false question and do something different depending on the answer

9 It's not a very fair game at the moment. Only one player can move the dot. Let's insert another **if statement** for the other direction. Test your game. You should be able to move the ball left and right. You must click on the preview window before the arrows keys will work.

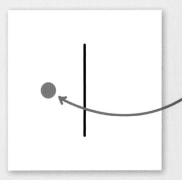

Pressing the left arrow key should move the dot 10 pixels to the left

```
  if (event.key === 'ArrowRight') {
    move(10)
  }
  if (event.key === 'ArrowLeft') {
    move(-10)
  }
})
```

A negative number moves the dot in the opposite direction of positive values

Here we're using the left arrow key instead of the right

10 We now just need to add some code to the end of the file that can check to see who wins. Let's add another function.

The **checkWinner** function looks at the red dot's position to see if it's left or right of the middle. It then tells you who's won

This first **if statement** checks if the dot's position **is bigger than (>)** the middle position

```
    move(-10)
  }
})

function checkWinner() {
  if (position > middle) {
    alert("Right wins!")
  }
  if (position < middle) {
    alert("Left wins!")
  }
  if (position === middle) {
    alert("It's a draw!")
  }
}
```

The last **if statement** checks if the position **is the same as (===)** the middle. If it is the same, you'll get a message to say it's a draw

This second **if statement** checks if the dot's position is **smaller than (<)** the middle

11 Almost there! Our new **checkWinner** function won't work until we write code to run it. Add this code to the end of your JavaScript file and then play the game.

An embedded page at mozillathimblelivepreview.net says:

It's a draw!

OK

```
    alert("It's a draw!")
  }
}

setTimeout(checkWinner, 10000)
```

To play again, refresh and then click on the preview page

setTimeout starts a timer. After 10,000 milliseconds (10 seconds), it runs the **checkWinner** function to see who's won. It then shows the winning message

PREVIEW ⟳ ☑ AUTO

Show what you know

1. Match each of these comparisons to their name.

===	Is smaller than
>	Is different from
<	Is the same as
! ==	Is bigger than

2. If you changed this code:

```
if (event.key === 'ArrowRight') {
    move(10)
} else if (event.key === 'ArrowLeft') {
    move(-10)
}
```

to this:

```
if (event.key === 'ArrowRight') {
    move(20)
} else if (event.key === 'ArrowLeft') {
    move(-10)
}
```

how would it change the game?

3. What is the name and argument of this function?

```
function sing(nameOfSong) {
    ...
}
```

4. Figure out who wins if the **checkWinner** function is run when

a. The position is equal to 100

b. The position is equal to 400

c. The position is equal to 275

Maze Challenge

Use JavaScript to make a fun maze. Draw a path on-screen, and see if your friends can find their way back to the start. But be careful—if they go outside the white line it's game over!

The black rectangle is your canvas

Draw your own winding path, such as this tree-shaped maze

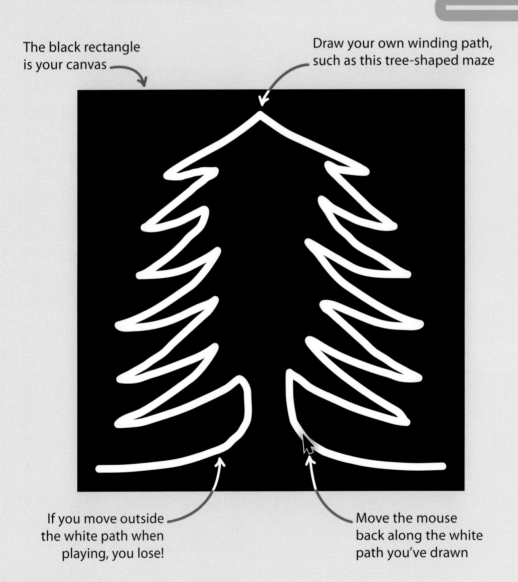

If you move outside the white path when playing, you lose!

Move the mouse back along the white path you've drawn

▲ What you do

Using HTML and JavaScript, you'll draw a white path on a black canvas using your mouse. Make it as winding and mazelike as you want. Then, see if you can carefully retrace your way back without straying outside the path.

Begin with HTML

As in our other projects, we begin with some HTML to set up our page. Copy the code in black exactly as it is in each of the steps. One tiny error may stop your code from working.

This maze is amazing!

1 Create a new project in Thimble. First, let's edit a few things in the code that's already in the HTML file. In the **body** element, change the code to what's shown below.

This line of code shows a heading on the page

```
</head>
<body>
  <h1>Maze Challenge</h1>
  <p>
    Click and drag to draw a path. Then try to move your
    mouse back to the start—but don't touch the edges!
  </p>
  <canvas width="500" height="500"></canvas>
  <script src="script.js"></script>
</body>
```

This line links the HTML file to the JavaScript file that we're about to create

Delete the original text that was here, and type in these instructions

2 Create a JavaScript file. Delete the code that's already there. First, let's set up the canvas in your JavaScript file, just like we did in the **Digital Painter** project. We want a black background for our game. Type this code into your file.

The canvas is the black square that you'll draw your maze on

```
var canvas = document.querySelector('canvas')
var ctx = canvas.getContext('2d')

ctx.fillStyle = 'black'
ctx.fillRect(0, 0, 500, 500)
```

3 Our game has two modes. We'll either be drawing a path or playing by navigating through the maze. Let's create some variables (see page 11) that will remember these modes.

These variables can be either true or false

```
ctx.fillStyle = 'black'
ctx.fillRect(0, 0, 500, 500)

var drawing = false
var playing = false
```

4 When we start pressing the mouse, we want to begin drawing the maze rather than playing on it. Add these lines of code. They create an event listener (see page 21) that changes our **drawing** and **playing** variables.

When the mouse is pressed down, we're in drawing mode rather than playing mode

```
var drawing = false
var playing = false

canvas.addEventListener('mousedown', function(event) {
  drawing = true
  playing = false
})
```

5 It's time to get ready to draw our maze. Insert this code between the last two lines from step 4.

First, we want to draw a black rectangle over anything that might already be on the screen

```
canvas.addEventListener('mousedown', function(event) {
  drawing = true
  playing = false

  ctx.fillRect(0, 0, 500, 500)

  ctx.lineWidth = 10
  ctx.lineCap = 'round'
  ctx.strokeStyle = 'white'

  ctx.beginPath()
  ctx.moveTo(event.offsetX, event.offsetY)
})
```

This code lets you begin drawing a line, called **Path** here, and moves the pen to where the mouse is

This code gets our pen ready for drawing the line

6 Let's add code for drawing the maze. Whenever we move the mouse—if we're in drawing mode—we want to draw the next bit of line. Add this code to the end of the file.

This code uses an **if statement**, which draws the next part of the line if we're in the drawing mode

```
ctx.beginPath()
ctx.moveTo(event.offsetX, event.offsetY)
})


canvas.addEventListener('mousemove', function(event) {
  if (drawing) {
    ctx.lineTo(event.offsetX, event.offsetY)
    ctx.stroke()
  }
})
```

Mouse events

Our program has three **mouse** events to "listen out" for. We've already used **mousedown** and **mousemove**. We're now about to add **mouseup**!

I can't get my mouse to move!!

7 Test your code! Click ↻ and then try clicking and dragging on the black square. Your mouse should draw a white line. However, when you release the mouse, the line keeps being drawn. Let's fix that with one final event listener. Add this code to the end of the file.

When you let go of the mouse button—the **mouseup** event—drawing mode is turned off and playing mode is turned on

```
    ctx.stroke()
  }
})


canvas.addEventListener('mouseup', function(event) {
  drawing = false
  playing = true
})
```

8 Insert these lines into the **mousemove** listener code from step 6. When we're in playing mode, it figures out if the mouse is inside the white line we drew. It remembers this in a variable called **insideLine**.

The variable **insideLine** asks whether **isPointInStroke**, which means: "Is the mouse inside the white line?" It remembers the answer

```
    ctx.stroke()
  }

  if (playing) {
    var insideLine =
      ctx.isPointInStroke(event.offsetX, event.offsetY)
  }
})
```

9 Let's add some code that ends the game if you stray outside the path. Insert these lines inside the code from step 8. Make sure you use the right number of **{ }** brackets!

An exclamation mark means **not**. These lines mean: "If the mouse is not in the line, end the game, show a message, and make the line red."

```
    var insideLine =
      ctx.isPointInStroke(event.offsetX, event.offsetY)

    if (!insideLine) {
      playing = false
      alert('You lose!')

      ctx.strokeStyle = 'red'
      ctx.stroke()
    }
  }
```

10 Refresh the page, and then click and drag to draw a path. Make sure you stay inside the black square. Next, guide the mouse back to the start without pressing down. If you stray from the path, you'll get a message. Click **OK** and the path will turn red. Refresh to play again.

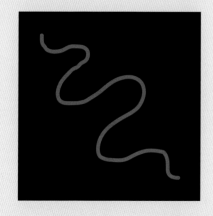

Try to keep inside the lines!

Show what you know

1. Draw a line to connect each event with its description.

mouseup   When you press the mouse

mousedown   When you move the mouse

mousemove   When you let go of the mouse

2. Rearrange the words below into a sentence to describe what this code says.

```
if (coldWeather) {
    wearCoat()
}
```

is cold   **then**   **the weather**   **a coat.**   **If**   **wear**

3. In step 5, we added this line of code: `ctx.lineWidth = 10`

If you changed the code to: `ctx.lineWidth = 20`

what effect would it have on the game for the player?

a. It would make the game easier to play.

b. It would make the game harder to play.

4. Find the mistake in this code.

```
if (musicPlaying) {
  if (gotTheMoves) {
    dance()
}
```

Hint: For JavaScript code to work, every **{** (opening bracket) needs a corresponding **}** (closing bracket).

5. What would happen if you changed the JavaScript code at the beginning to this?

```
var canvas = document.querySelector('canvas')
var ctx = canvas.getContext('2d')

ctx.fillStyle = 'purple'
ctx.fillRect(0, 0, 400, 400)
```

Solutions

Good job! You've now completed all the projects! Time to check your **Show what you know** answers.

Let's give them the answers!

pages 8–16 Digital Painter

1. HTML stands for **H**yper**T**ext **M**arkup **L**anguage.

2. Circle the correct answer.
The (**canvas**)/ **variable** is an empty space we can paint on. JavaScript code tells the **element** /(**context**) what to paint.

3. Match these canvas functions to their definitions.

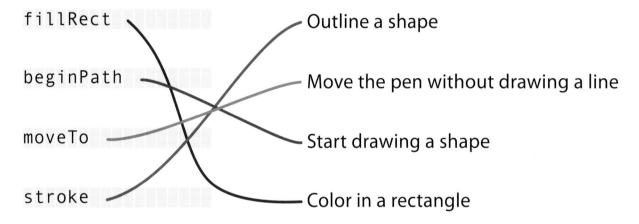

fillRect — Outline a shape

beginPath — Move the pen without drawing a line

moveTo — Start drawing a shape

stroke — Color in a rectangle

4. A **variable** is used to store **information** that we need in our **program**.

5. **b.** Diamond

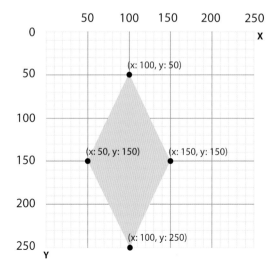

1. Circle the correct answers.

a. You can use the **getUserMedia** / **getUserCamera** command in JavaScript to ask for permission to use your webcam.

b. By adding a **layer** / **filter** to the video you can create your own special effects.

2. Draw a line to connect each piece of code to its description

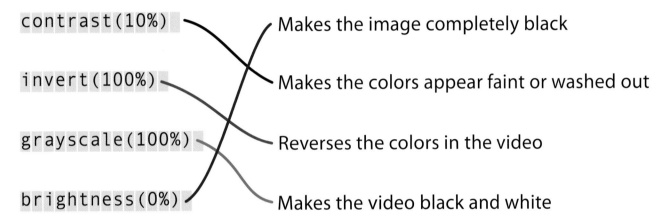

```
contrast(10%)
```
Makes the image completely black

```
invert(100%)
```
Makes the colors appear faint or washed out

```
grayscale(100%)
```
Reverses the colors in the video

```
brightness(0%)
```
Makes the video black and white

3. The new **Sepia** option adds a reddish-brown filter that can make a video look old.

4. The closing tag of the **Apple Juice option** element was incorrect. It was missing a forward slash.

```
<option>Apple Juice</option>
```

5. a. Event listener

1. Match each of these comparisons to their name.

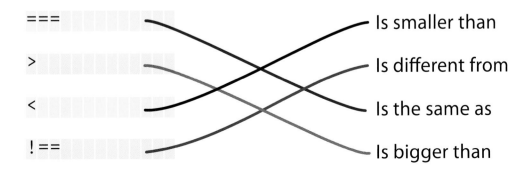

```
===
```
Is smaller than

```
>
```
Is different from

```
<
```
Is the same as

```
!==
```
Is bigger than

2. Changing **move (10)** to **move (20)** would make the game much easier for the right player, since each time the right arrow key is pressed the red dot would move twice as far to the right.

3. The name of the function is **sing** and the argument is **nameOfSong**.

4. Figure out who wins if the **checkWinner** function is run when

a. The position is equal to 100   **Left wins**

b. The position is equal to 400   **Right wins**

c. The position is equal to 275   **Right wins**

pages 32–37 Maze Challenge

1. Draw a line to connect each event with its description.

```
mouseup          When you press the mouse
mousedown        When you move the mouse
mousemove        When you let go of the mouse
```

2. The code says:

If the weather is cold then wear a coat.

3. a. It would make the game easier to play.
Changing this code increases the width of the white line from 10 to 20 pixels. If the line is wider, it is easier for the player to stay on the path.

4. There are two **{** (opening brackets) but just one **}** (closing bracket). The code needs an extra **}** to work.

```
if (musicPlaying) {
   if (gotTheMoves) {
      dance()
   }
}
```
— A closing bracket was missing

5. The rectangle would be smaller—only 400 by 400 pixels—and purple rather than black if you made those changes.